Handmade Happiness

Trinkets and Treasures for Quilters to Enjoy

Jina Barney and Lori Woods of *Poppie Cotton*

Martingale
Create with Confidence

Handmade Happiness: Trinkets and Treasures
for Quilters to Enjoy
© 2021 by Jina Barney and Lori Woods

Martingale®
18939 120th Ave. NE, Ste. 101
Bothell, WA 98011-9511 USA
ShopMartingale.com

Printed in Hong Kong
26 25 24 23 22 21   8 7 6 5 4 3 2 1

Library of Congress Cataloging-in-Publication Data
is available upon request.

ISBN: 978-1-68356-150-7

MISSION STATEMENT

We empower makers who use fabric and yarn
to make life more enjoyable.

CREDITS

**PUBLISHER AND
CHIEF VISIONARY OFFICER**
Jennifer Erbe Keltner

CONTENT DIRECTOR
Karen Costello Soltys

DESIGN MANAGER
Adrienne Smitke

TECHNICAL EDITOR
Elizabeth Beese

PRODUCTION MANAGER
Regina Girard

COPY EDITOR
Durby Peterson

**COVER AND
BOOK DESIGNER**
Mia Mar

TECHNICAL ILLUSTRATOR
Sandy Loi

PHOTOGRAPHER
Brent Kane

WATERCOLOR ILLUSTRATOR
Lori Woods

SPECIAL THANKS
*Some of the photography for this book was taken at
Lori Clark's the FarmHouse Cottage
in Snohomish, Washington.*

Contents

Introduction

It all began with a love of the creative process, a new friendship, and a common goal of bringing something completely fresh and different to our new venture and company, Poppie Cotton. We love the creative process—it's where our passion ignites and where the lovely Poppie Cotton products are made. We're two friends who have a deep desire to inspire your creativity by making and embellishing pieces that are sure to delight. Truly, this process never seems to be finished as we fuss over every detail of each project again and again. All the projects in this book have been made with the hope that as you turn each page, you'll see the dedication to detail in every project.

We hope that you'll also experience the fun and delightful process of creating . . . choosing your special materials and embellishments, adding details to every stitch, and if you're like us, making two of everything—one to keep as a sweet, favorite treasure and one to give as a special, handmade gift.

You will learn techniques such as embroidery, stamping, machine and hand stitching, and embellishing. You will become the star as you develop a love for these sweet skills. The projects are intended to be made by anyone, even beginners, ensuring that you feel comfortable as you find your own creative voice. You will get to select materials, gather buttons and trims, learn to place a zipper, sew simple stitches by hand, and finish sweet and beautiful projects.

This is a process, so allow yourself the mistakes of discovery and learning. Be cautious and yet look forward as you move toward your finished creations. It is our hope that you'll enjoy your journey as you turn each page, because happiness is handmade!

Jina and Lori

Stitch It with Love

Keep your sewing needles safely tucked inside a case that's perfect for projects on the go. The interior pocket neatly holds embroidery floss, needle threaders, and more.

Small Needle Case

Finished size: 3¾" × 4½" (closed)

Materials

Yardage is based on 42"-wide fabric.

❋ ¼ yard *total* of assorted prints in white, pink, and aqua for needle case outside, lining, and pocket

❋ 1 strip, 2½" × 42", of coral print for binding

❋ 8" × 9" piece of batting

❋ 7" × 8" piece of light pink felted wool for pages

❋ ¼ yard of light pink rickrack, ½" wide, for pocket embellishment

❋ ½ yard of light pink ribbon, ½" wide, for tie

❋ 7 paper hexagon pieces, ½" size (*OR* sturdy paper if making your own)

❋ 1 paper hexagon piece, ¾" size (*OR* sturdy paper if making your own)

❋ Water-soluble glue

Cutting

All measurements include ¼" seam allowances.

From the assorted prints, cut:

1 piece, 5" × 8" (lining)

2 pieces, 4" × 5" (front and back)

2 pieces, 2¾" × 7½" (pocket)

1 strip, 1" × 5" (spine)

1 square, 2" × 2" (medium hexagon)

7 squares, 1½" × 1½" (small hexagons)

From the batting, cut:

1 piece, 5" × 8"

1 piece, 2¾" × 7½"

From the light pink wool, cut:

2 pieces, 3½" × 6"

From the ribbon, cut:

2 pieces, 8" long

Assembling the Small Needle Case

Use a ¼" seam allowance and sew right sides together unless otherwise specified. Press the seam allowances in the directions indicated by the arrows.

1 Sew together the print 4" × 5" pieces and 1" × 5" strip as shown to make the needle case cover.

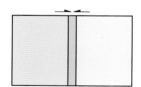

Make 1 small needle case cover,
8" × 5".

2 With the fabric right side out, sandwich the batting 5" × 8" piece between the needle case cover and the lining 5" × 8" piece. Quilt as desired. The featured project is machine stitched with horizontal parallel lines every ¼". Trim the quilted unit to 4½" × 7½", including seam allowances.

6 Use the remainder of the coral 2½"-wide strip to bind all edges.

7 Center the light pink wool 3½" × 6" pieces in the middle of the quilted outside piece, on top of the pocket. Stitch down the center. Backstitch at each end to secure.

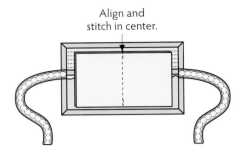

Align and stitch in center.

3 With the fabric right side out, sandwich the batting 2¾" × 7½" piece between the print 2¾" × 7½" pieces to make the pocket. Machine quilt parallel horizontal lines about ¼" apart. Baste the rickrack even with one long straight edge of the pocket (this will be the top).

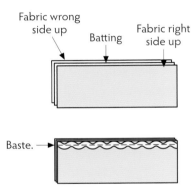

Fabric wrong side up

Batting

Fabric right side up

Baste.

4 Use the coral 2½"-wide strip to bind the top edge of the pocket.

5 Aligning the bottom edges, place the pocket right side up on the inside of the needle case cover. Baste the pocket in place. Line up the ribbon ends with the raw edges of sides of the pocket, with the remainder of the ribbon facing the inside of the needle case. Baste in place.

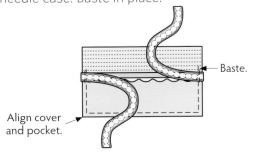

Baste.

Align cover and pocket.

Embellishing the Small Needle Case

1 Refer to "English Paper Piecing" on page 78 to prepare seven small hexagons using the print 1½" squares and ½" paper hexagons and prepare one medium hexagon using the print 2" square and ¾" paper hexagon. If you're making your own paper hexagons, the patterns are on page 11. Lay out the prepared ½" hexagons in a flower shape. Join the pieces, starting by sewing the center hexagon to one outer hexagon. Join all outer hexagons to the center hexagon, then join the outer hexagons to each other.

2 Remove the papers from the flower unit. Center it on the front cover of the needle case and hand sew in place. Center the prepared ¾" hexagon on the back cover and hand sew in place.

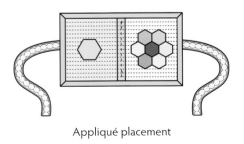

Appliqué placement

Large Needle Case

Finished size: 4¾" × 5½" (closed)

Materials

Yardage is based on 42"-wide fabric.

❋ ⅓ yard *total* of assorted prints in white, pink, and aqua for needle case outside, lining, and pocket

❋ 2 strips, 2½" × 42", of aqua print for binding

❋ 11" × 12" piece of batting

❋ 9" × 10" piece of coral felted wool for pages

❋ ⅓ yard of light pink rickrack, ½" wide, for pocket embellishment

❋ ½ yard of light pink ribbon, ½" wide, for tie

❋ 1 paper hexagon piece, ¾" size (*OR* sturdy paper if making your own)

❋ 4" × 4" square of fusible fleece

❋ Embroidery floss in aqua, dusty green, and fuchsia

❋ Fine-point permanent pen *OR* Tranquil-i-Tea Collection stamps and permanent-ink stamp pad*

❋ Water-soluble glue

❋ Embroidery needle

The project shown features the Stamp & Stitch Tranquil-i-Tea Collection stamps available from Poppie Cotton. See "Resources," page 80.

Cutting

All measurements include ¼" seam allowances.

From the assorted prints, cut:

1 piece, 6" × 10" (lining)

2 pieces, 5" × 6" (front and back)

2 pieces, 3½" × 9½" (pocket)

1 strip, 1" × 6" (spine)

1 square, 5" × 5" (large hexagon)

1 square, 2" × 2" (medium hexagon)

From the batting, cut:

1 piece, 6" × 10"

1 piece, 3½" × 9½"

From the coral wool, cut:

2 pieces, 4½" × 8½"

From the ribbon, cut:

2 pieces, 8" long

From the fusible fleece, cut:

1 large hexagon (page 11)

Assembling the Large Needle Case

Use a ¼" seam allowance and sew right sides together unless otherwise specified. Press the seam allowances in the directions indicated by the arrows.

1 Sew together the print 5" × 6" pieces and 1" × 6" strip as shown to make the large needle case cover.

Make 1 large needle case cover, 10" × 6".

2 Using the needle case cover and the batting and lining 6" × 10" pieces, refer to step 2 of "Assembling the Small Needle Case" on page 7 to quilt the needle case. Trim to 5½" × 9½", including seam allowances.

3 Using the batting and print 3½" × 9½" pieces, rickrack, and aqua print 2½"-wide strips, refer to steps 3 and 4 of "Assembling the Small Needle Case" on page 7 to make and bind the pocket. Refer to step 5 and to add the pocket and ribbons to the needle case.

4 Use the remainder of the aqua 2½"-wide strips to make binding. Bind all edges.

5 Center the coral wool 4½" × 8½" pieces in the middle of the quilted outside piece, on top of the pocket. Stitch down the center. Backstitch at each end to secure.

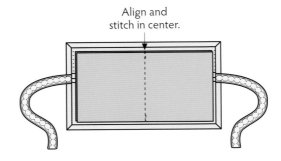

Align and stitch in center.

Embellishing the Large Needle Case

Use two strands of embroidery floss unless otherwise stated. Refer to "Embroidery Stitches" on page 79 and the pattern on page 11 as needed.

1 Refer to "English Paper Piecing" on page 78 to prepare one medium hexagon using the print 2" square and ¾" paper hexagon. Remove the paper. If you're making your own paper hexagon, the pattern is on page 11.

2 Using a light box or sunny window, trace the embroidery design with a permanent pen onto the print 5" square, centering the design. Or, if you're using the Tranquil-i-tea Collection stamps, stamp the design instead.

3 With its fusible side down, center the fusible fleece large hexagon over the back of the traced design. Stitching through all layers, embroider the design. Use dusty green floss to backstitch the individual leaf patterns and stems and use lazy daisy stitches on the flower stem and sprig of leaves. Use fuchsia floss to backstitch the word, make lazy daisy stitches for the flower petals, and stitch a French knot in the center of the flower. Use aqua floss to make star stitches and French knots.

4 Trim the excess fabric, leaving generous ¼" seam allowances. Turn the seam allowances to the back of the fusible fleece and stitch in place with a running stitch.

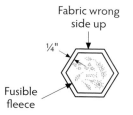

Fabric wrong side up

¼"

Fusible fleece

5 Center the embroidered hexagon on the front cover of the needle book and the prepared ¾" hexagon on the back cover. Hand sew in place.

Fabric right side up

Fusible fleece behind fabric

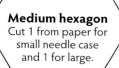

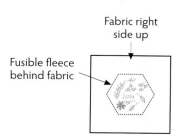

Medium hexagon
Cut 1 from paper for small needle case and 1 for large.

Small hexagon

Cut 7 from paper for small needle case (none for large).

Large hexagon
Cut 1 from fusible fleece for large needle case (none for small).

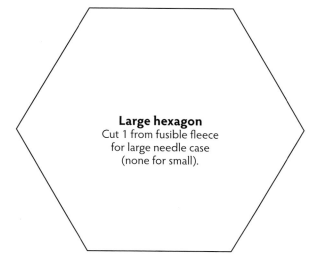

love

Embroidery pattern

Embroidery Key

- - - - - Backstitch

● French knot

⌒ Lazy daisy

✱ Star stitch

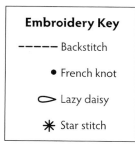

Wool Zipper Pouches

With a strawberry here, a chicken there, and a great mushroom for good measure, these pouches are packed with personality. Fill with tiny treasures, zip 'em up, and enjoy!

Finished Size: 5½" × 4½"

Materials

Yields 1 pouch.

Chicken Pouch

* 6" × 10" piece of green felted wool for pouch
* 3" × 3" square of ivory felted wool for chicken
* 1½" × 1½" square of red felted wool for waddle and comb
* 2" × 2" square of pink felted wool for wing
* Embroidery floss in black, ivory, pink, and red

Strawberry Pouch

* 6" × 10" piece of pink felted wool for pouch
* 3" × 3" square of red felted wool for strawberry
* 3" × 3" square of green felted wool for stem
* Embroidery floss in green, pink, and red

Mushroom Pouch

* 6" × 10" piece of blue felted wool for pouch
* 1¼" × 2" piece of ivory felted wool for mushroom stem
* 2½" × 3" piece of red felted wool for mushroom cap
* 2½" × 2½" square of pink felted wool for spots
* Embroidery floss in ivory, pink, and red

All Pouches

You will need the following materials for each pouch.

* Zipper, 7" long
* Scrap of fabric selvage, 1" × 3" or larger, with a word printed on it
* Chenille needle, size #20 or #22
* Freezer paper

Appliquéing the Pouch Body

Use two strands of embroidery floss unless otherwise stated. Refer to "Embroidery Stitches" on page 79 and the pattern on page 15 as needed.

1   Referring to "Wool Appliqué" on page 78, trace the patterns for the chosen appliqués on page 15 onto the freezer paper and prepare the wool shapes.

2   Referring to the diagram for placement, position the wool pieces for the chicken, strawberry, or mushroom on one end of the wool 6" × 10" background piece and pin in place; center the designs across the 6" width.

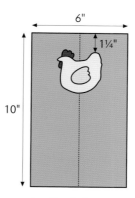

Appliqué placement

3   For all pieces except the spots on the mushroom, blanket stitch the pieces in place, matching the thread color to the motif. For the chicken, use black thread to make a French knot for an eye. For the strawberry, use pink floss to make French knots for seeds. For the mushroom, use pink floss to cross-stitch each spot in place on the cap.

Assembling the Pouch

Use a ¼" seam allowance and sew right sides together unless otherwise specified.

1 Fold under ¼" on the top raw edge of the selvage scrap. Topstitch in place. Fold the rectangle in half widthwise and place the raw edges on the right-hand side of the pouch body, with the fold toward the inside of the pouch body and the top even with the top of the appliqué. Baste in place.

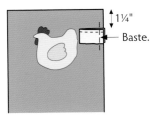

2 With right sides together, center the zipper on the top of the appliquéd wool piece. Machine stitch the wool piece to one side of the zipper. Finger-press the zipper up and away from the wool piece, pressing the seam allowances toward the wool piece. Topstitch close to the seam to secure the seam allowances.

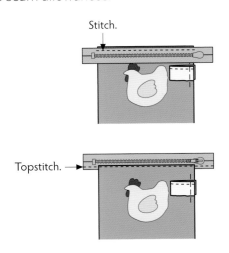

3 Bring the other short edge of the wool pouch to the remaining edge of the zipper with right sides together. Machine stitch in place.

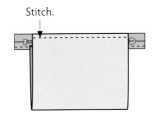

4 Finger-press the zipper up and away from the wool piece, pressing the seam allowances toward the wool piece. Topstitch close to the seam to secure the seam allowances. Move the zipper pull to the middle of the pouch.

5 With the zipper at the top, sew the side seams, backstitching across the zipper tape to secure it. Trim the zipper ends and turn the pouch right side out.

Appliqué patterns do not include seam allowances.

Wing
Make 1 from pink wool.

Stem
Make 1 from green wool.

Waddle/Comb
Make 1 from red wool.

Chicken
Make 1 from ivory wool.

Strawberry
Make 1 from red wool.

Mushroom cap
Make 1 from red wool.

Mushroom stem
Make 1 from ivory wool.

Large spot
Make 3 from pink wool.

Small spot
Make 2 from pink wool.

Little Paper Tags

Tag, you're it! Create cheery decorative tags to use as gift labels, bookmarks, and bowl fillers. Each sturdy tag is quick to make and conveys its own simple message.

Finished size: 1¼" × 5½" (excluding tie)

Materials

Yields 10 tags.

* 1 sheet, 8½" × 11", of heavyweight light brown cardstock for tags

* Scraps of assorted cotton fabrics for embellishment

* 2¾ yards of jute cord for tie

* 10 eyelets in assorted colors

* Eyelet setting tool

* Pinking shears or rotary cutter with pinking blade

* Alphabet *OR* word rubber stamps, about ¼" tall

* Permanent-ink stamp pad in sepia

Cutting

From the light brown cardstock, cut:

10 rectangles, 1¼" × 5½"

From the assorted cotton fabrics, use pinking shears or a pinking blade to cut:

10 rectangles, 1¼" wide × 4" to 4½" long

From the jute cord, cut:

10 pieces, 9" long

Making the Tags

1 Refer to the photo on page 16 to stamp the desired word in the left-hand 3" of each cardstock rectangle.

2 Fold a fabric rectangle in half widthwise and place it over the right-hand end of a cardstock rectangle. Machine stitch ¼" from the short pinked ends to secure the fabric. Repeat for each tag.

3 On the fabric-covered end of a tag, poke a small hole ½" from the end. Insert an eyelet from the front (stamped side) of the tag and use an eyelet setter to set the eyelet. Thread a piece of jute through the eyelet and tie the ends in a knot. Repeat for each tag.

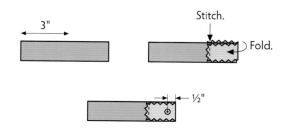

Bow Scrunchie

Make scrunchies for all seasons—and give them as gifts for any reason! Let your creativity shine with comfy fabric scrunchies that are as fun to stitch as they are to wear.

Finished Size: Approximately 7" diameter (excluding bow)

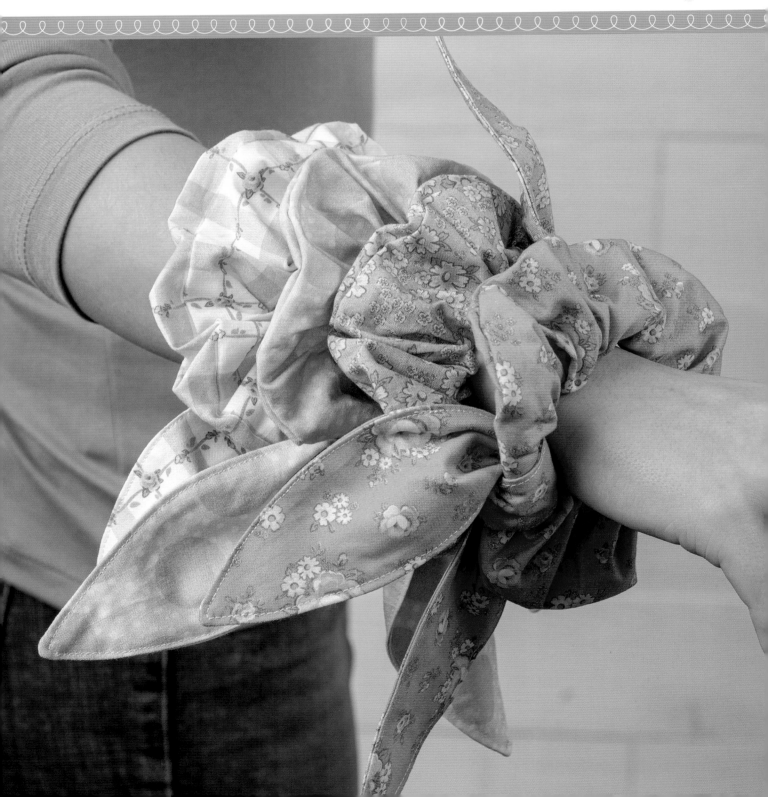

Materials

Yields 1 scrunchie. Fat quarters measure 18" × 22".

❊ 1 fat quarter of pink OR aqua print for scrunchie

❊ 8" length of elastic, ¼" wide

❊ Cardstock OR template plastic

Cutting

All measurements include ¼" seam allowances. Trace the bow pattern on page 20 onto cardstock or template plastic and cut it out. Use the template to cut the bows from the fabric indicated below.

From the pink OR aqua print, cut:

2 bows*

1 strip, 5" × 22"

*Be sure to place the marked edge on the fabric fold.

Assembling the Bow

Use a ¼" seam allowance and sew right sides together unless otherwise specified.

1 Layer the two bow pieces. Sew around the perimeter, leaving a 1" opening along one side. Clip the pointed ends to lessen fabric bulk in the points.

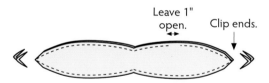

Leave 1" open. Clip ends.

2 Turn the bow right side out through the opening and press flat. Topstitch close to the edge.

Make 1 bow.

Assembling the Scrunchie

1 Fold under ½" on one short edge of the pink or aqua 5" × 22" strip. Then fold the strip in half lengthwise with right sides together. Sew together the long raw edges to make a tube.

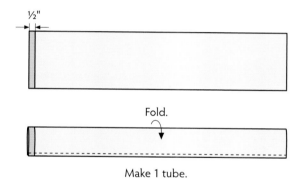

½"

Fold.

Make 1 tube.

2 Turn the tube right side out but do not press flat. With a safety pin, thread the elastic through the folded end of the tube. Pin one end of the elastic so it won't pull through. Once the elastic is all the way through the tube, overlap the elastic ends by ½" and zigzag the ends together.

Zigzag stitch.

3 Insert the raw edge of the tube about ½" inside the folded edge of the tube. Zigzag across the opening.

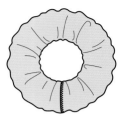

Make 1 scrunchie.

4 Refer to the photo on page 18 to tie the bow around the zigzagged seam to complete the scrunchie.

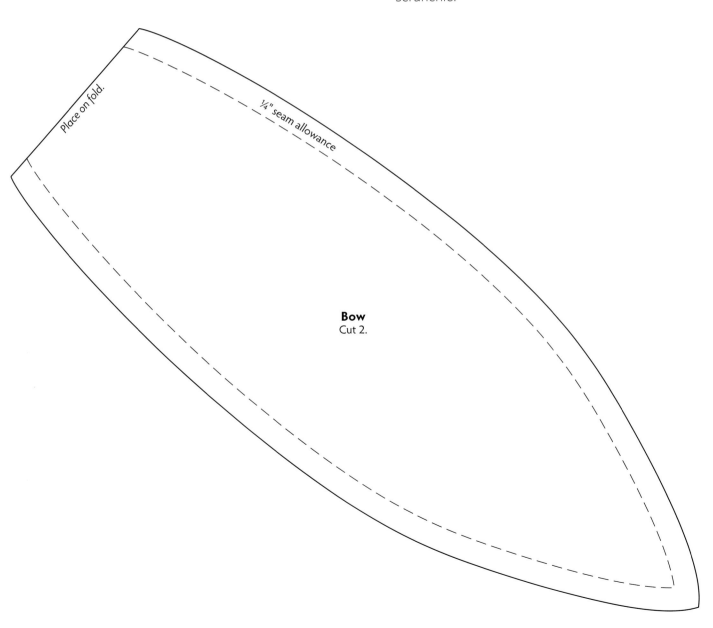

Place on fold.

¼" seam allowance

Bow
Cut 2.

Fabric Gift Boxes

Pamper your loved ones with a fabric box that's as sweet as any cargo it carries. Ideal for small items such as candy, scented soaps, or tea bags, each box is a gift in itself.

Finished Size: Small, 3" × 3" × 3"
Finished Size: Large, 3½" × 4" × 3"

Materials

Yields 1 gift box (small or large). Fat eighths measure 9" × 22".

* 1 fat eighth of main print for gift box outside

* 1 fat eighth of coordinating print for lining

* Scrap of coordinating print for tab

* 1 strip, 2½" × 42", of coordinating print for binding

* 7" × 12" piece of batting

* Scrap of selvage with word printed on it (optional)

* ½ yard of ball trim, ¾" wide (optional)

* Wonder Clips (optional)

Two Sizes, Two Finishes

We've not only provided instructions for two sizes of these adorable fabric boxes but also shown you two ways to finish them. Regardless of which size you make, you can add the purchased pom-pom trim—or not!

Cutting

All measurements include ¼" seam allowances.

Small Box

From the main print, cut:
1 piece, 6" × 10"

From the lining fabric, cut:
1 piece, 6" × 10"

From the scrap, cut:
1 piece, 2½" × 3"

From the binding strip, cut:
1 strip, 2½" × 11½"

From the batting, cut:
2 pieces, 6" × 10"

From the ball trim, cut:
1 piece, 12" long

Large Box

From the main print, cut:
1 piece, 7" × 12"

From the lining fabric, cut:
1 piece, 7" × 12"

From the scrap, cut:
1 piece, 2½" × 3"

From the binding strip, cut:
1 strip, 2½" × 13½"

From the batting, cut:
2 pieces, 7" × 12"

From the ball trim, cut:
1 piece, 14" long

Assembling the Small Gift Box

Use a ¼" seam allowance and sew right sides together unless otherwise specified.

1 Layer the main print 6" × 10" piece right side up on one batting 6" × 10" piece. Baste together around all edges, ⅛" from the edge.

Make 1 quilted box body, 6" × 10".

2 With wrong sides together, fold the quilted piece in half widthwise. Cut out each bottom corner as shown.

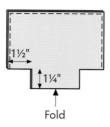

1½"

1¼"

Fold

3 Fold the print 2½" × 3" piece in half lengthwise and press; unfold. Fold each raw edge inward to meet at the pressed centerline, then fold in half on the centerline. Press. Topstitch close to the edge to complete the tab.

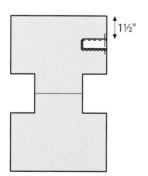

4 Unfold the unit from step 2. Turn under the edges of the selvage scrap and position it 1½" from the upper-right edge. Hand or machine sew in place. Fold the tab in half and position the raw edges of the tab on top of the selvage. Baste the tab raw ends to the box body within the seam allowance.

1½"

5 Refold the box body in half again with right sides together. Sew the side seams.

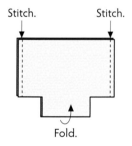

Stitch.   Stitch.

Fold.

6 Press the side seam allowances open. To box the bottom corners, bring the bottom pressed centerline up and align it with a side seam. Sew the raw edges together. Repeat for the remaining corner.

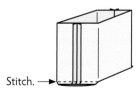

Stitch. →

7 Turn the box body right side out and press the corners out.

8 Repeat steps 1, 2, 5, and 6 with the 6" × 10" lining piece and remaining batting piece. With wrong sides together, insert the lining into the box body. Match the seams and pin or use Wonder Clips to secure.

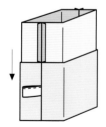

9 Join the short ends of the binding strip and press the seam allowances open. Fold the resulting tube in half with wrong sides together.

10 Place the binding over the outside of the box body, aligning the raw edges at the top and matching the seams. Use a ¼" seam to sew the binding in place. If you're adding the optional ball trim, sew it in place on the lining side of the box, with the pom-poms extending down toward the bottom of the bag, and sew in place.

11 Bring the folded edge of the binding to the lining side and topstitch to secure. Fold down the top edge of the box body so the binding is on the outside.

Assembling the Large Gift Box

Using the 7" × 12" fabric and batting pieces instead of the smaller pieces, repeat the assembly steps for the small box to make the large box.

Heartfelt Quilts

Sometimes the best quilts come in small sizes! Create a tiny stitchery and a welcoming table topper, each with simple patchwork in a heartwarming design.

Mini Quilt

Finished size: 6½" × 6½"

Mini Quilt

Materials

Yardage is based on 42"-wide fabric.

❋ ⅛ yard of linen solid for background

❋ ¼ yard *total* of assorted prints in turquoise, pink, and white for pieced heart

❋ 1 strip, 2½" × 42", of pink-and-white stripe for binding

❋ 8" × 8" square of fabric for backing

❋ 8" × 8" square of batting

❋ 2" × 2" square of light coral felted wool for heart appliqué

❋ Embroidery floss in coral, light coral, and pink

❋ Scrap of fabric selvage with word or phrase printed on it (optional)

❋ Freezer paper

Cutting

All measurements include ¼" seam allowances.

From the linen solid, cut:

2 squares, 3½" × 3½"

2 squares, 1⅞" × 1⅞"

From the assorted turquoise, pink, and white prints, cut:

2 squares, 1⅞" × 1⅞"

26 squares, 1½" × 1½"

Assembling the Quilt Top

Use a ¼" seam allowance and sew right sides together. Press the seam allowances in the directions indicated by the arrows.

1 Draw a diagonal line from corner to corner on the wrong side of each linen solid 1⅞" square and 3½" square. Place a marked 1⅞" square right sides together with a print 1⅞" square. Sew ¼" from both sides of the drawn line. Cut the unit apart on the

drawn line to make two half-square-triangle units measuring 1½" square, including seam allowances. Make four half-square-triangle units.

Make 4 units
1½" × 1½".

2 Arrange the four half-square-triangle units and 26 print 1½" squares in six rows. Sew together the pieces in each row. Join the rows to make a heart unit.

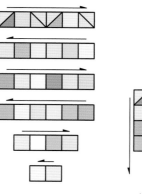

Make 1 heart unit.

3 Place a marked 3½" square right sides together with the lower-left corner of the heart unit, lining up the raw edges. Sew on the drawn line. Trim the seam allowances to ¼" and press the resulting triangle open.

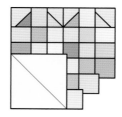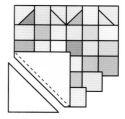

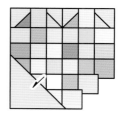

5 Refer to "Wool Appliqué" on page 78 to trace the heart pattern for the appliqué below onto the freezer paper and prepare the wool shape. Position the wool heart on the quilt top as desired and whipstitch in place with light coral floss. Use coral floss to cross-stitch Xs on the heart.

Finishing

Use two strands of embroidery floss. Refer to "Embroidery Stitches" on page 79 as needed. For help with any of the following steps, go to ShopMartingale.com/HowtoQuilt for free, illustrated instructions.

1 Layer the quilt top with the batting and backing. Baste the layers together.

2 Quilt as desired. The quilt shown is machine quilted on either side of the horizontal seams. It is then hand quilted with a crosshatch design through the pieced heart. Running stitches and cross-stitches are hand embroidered in the linen solid background using pink embroidery floss.

3 Turn under the edges of the selvage scrap and position it on the quilt top as desired. Hand or machine sew in place.

4 Trim the batting and backing even with the quilt top.

5 Use the pink-and-white stripe 2½"-wide strip to make binding. Attach the binding to the quilt.

4 Add the remaining marked 3½" square to the lower-right corner of the heart unit as before to complete the quilt top. The quilt top should be 6½" square, including seam allowances.

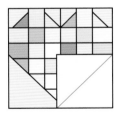 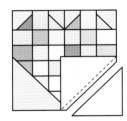

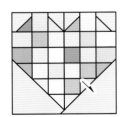

Quilt top,
6½" × 6½"

Heart
Make 1 from light
coral wool.

Heartfelt Quilts

Table Topper
Finished size: 16½" × 16½"

Table Topper

Materials

Yardage is based on 42"-wide fabric. Fat quarters measure 18" × 22".

⁕ ⅓ yard of mottled pink print for background and border

⁕ ⅓ yard *total* of assorted prints in red, pink, and white for pieced heart

⁕ ¼ yard of black-and-white stripe for binding

⁕ 20" × 20" square of fabric for backing

⁕ 20" × 20" square of batting

⁕ Embroidery floss in red

Cutting

All measurements include ¼" seam allowances.

From the mottled pink print, cut:

2 strips, 2½" × 16½"

2 pieces, 2½" × 6½"

2 pieces, 2½" × 4½"

5 squares, 2⅞" × 2⅞"

8 squares, 2½" × 2½"

From the assorted red, pink, and white prints, cut:

5 squares, 2⅞" × 2⅞"

20 squares, 2½" × 2½"

From the black-and-white stripe, cut:

2 strips, 2½" × 42"

Assembling the Quilt Top

Use a ¼" seam allowance and sew right sides together. Press the seam allowances in the directions indicated by the arrows.

1 Draw a diagonal line from corner to corner on the wrong side of each mottled pink 2⅞" square. Place a marked square right sides together with one of the assorted print 2⅞" squares. Sew ¼" from both sides of the drawn line. Cut the unit apart on the drawn line to make two half-square-triangle units, each 2½" square, including seam allowances. Make 10 half-square-triangle units.

Make 10 units,
2½" × 2½".

2 Arrange all remaining mottled pink pieces (two 2½" × 16½" strips, eight 2½" squares, two 2½" × 4½" pieces, and two 2½" × 6½" pieces), the 10 half-square-triangle units, and 20 assorted print 2½" squares in eight rows. Sew together the pieces in each row. Join the rows to complete the quilt top. It should be 16½" square, including seam allowances.

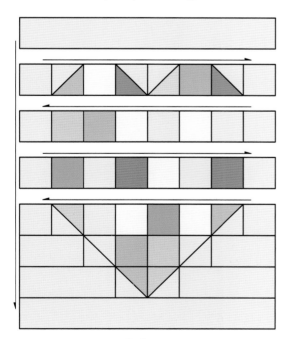

Quilt top,
16½" × 16½"

Cross My Heart

One of the most charming details about this little quilt is the embroidery floss quilting. We used basic cross-stitches and running stitches, with a few star stitches tossed in for good measure. See "Embroidery Stitches" on page 79. Even if you've never stitched by hand before, now's your chance!

Finishing

For help with any of the following steps, go to ShopMartingale.com/HowtoQuilt for free, illustrated instructions.

1 Layer the quilt top with the batting and backing. Baste the layers together.

2 Quilt as desired. The quilt shown is machine quilted with a crosshatch through the pieced heart and echoing heart shapes about ⅜" apart in the background. Then a variety of stitches, such as running stitches, cross-stitches, and star stitches, are hand embroidered on the quilt top using red embroidery floss.

3 Trim the batting and backing even with the quilt top.

4 Use the black-and-white stripe 2½"-wide strips to make binding. Attach the binding to the quilt.

Hexie Sewing Tools

Enjoy making pincushions and scissors fobs as gifts for your friends or for yourself—they're so addictive and adorable, you won't be able to stop stitching them!

Pincushion

ℓℓℓℓℓℓℓℓℓℓ

Finished size: Approximately 3½" diameter

Materials

Yields 1 pincushion.

* 7 squares, 1½" × 1½", of assorted prints for hexagons

* 1 square, 8" × 8", of coordinating print for pincushion top

* 7 paper hexagon pieces, ½" size (*OR* sturdy paper if making your own)

* Cardstock *OR* template plastic

* Water-soluble glue

* Polyester fiberfill *OR* other pincushion filling

* Mini tart tin or cupcake tin with base approximately 2" diameter

* Hot-glue gun and glue sticks

Cutting

Trace the circle pattern on page 36 onto cardstock or template plastic and cut it out. Use the template to cut the circle from the fabric indicated below.

From the coordinating print, cut:

1 circle

Assembling the Pincushion

Use a ¼" seam allowance and sew right sides together.

1 Refer to "English Paper Piecing" on page 78 to prepare seven hexagons using the print 1½" squares and ½" paper hexagons. If making your own paper hexagons, the pattern is on page 36. Lay out the prepared hexagons in a flower shape. Join the pieces, starting by sewing the center hexagon to one outer hexagon. Join all outer hexagons to the center hexagon, then join the outer hexagons to each other.

Make 1 flower unit.

2 Remove the papers from the flower unit. Center it on the right side of the coordinating print circle and hand sew in place.

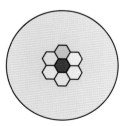

Sew flower unit to fabric circle.

3 Use a doubled thread and stitches about ¼" long to sew a running stitch ¼" from the outside edge of the circle.

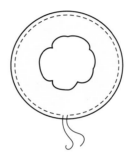

4 Gather the threads and then stuff the center of the circle with stuffing. Continue to tighten the stitches and stuff firmly. Secure the thread with a knot.

5 Hot glue the bottom of the pincushion into the tin.

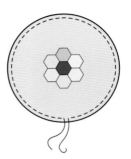

It's All in the Details

If you're giving the pincushion as a gift, make it extra special by making some cute pins. Thread a bead or two onto a ball-head pin and superglue in place.

Assembling the Scissors Fob

Use a ¼" seam allowance and sew right sides together unless otherwise specified. Press the seam allowances in the directions indicated by the arrows.

1 Refer to step 1 of "Assembling the Pincushion" on page 33 to prepare 14 hexagons and make two flower units.

2 Fold the fabric strip in half and press; unfold. Fold each raw edge inward to meet at the pressed centerline, then fold in half on the centerline. Press. Topstitch close to the edge to complete the tie. If desired, use two strands of embroidery floss to sew a running stitch over the machine stitching.

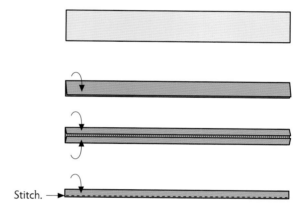

Stitch. ➤

Scissors Fob

Finished size: 2½" × 2⅝" (excluding tie)

Materials

* 14 squares, 1½" × 1½", of coordinating prints for hexagons

* 1 strip, 2" × 14", of coordinating fabric for tie

* 14 paper hexagon pieces, ½" size (*OR* sturdy paper if making your own)

* Embroidery floss in coordinating color (optional)

* Water-soluble glue

3 Leave the papers inside the flower units and layer with wrong sides together. Fold the tie in half and encase the raw ends between the flower units. Whipstitch the edges of the flower units together with tiny stitches.

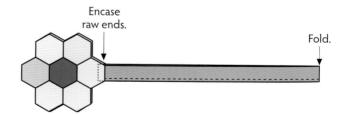

Encase raw ends.

Fold.

4 Use a lark's head knot to secure the fob tie around one handle of your scissors.

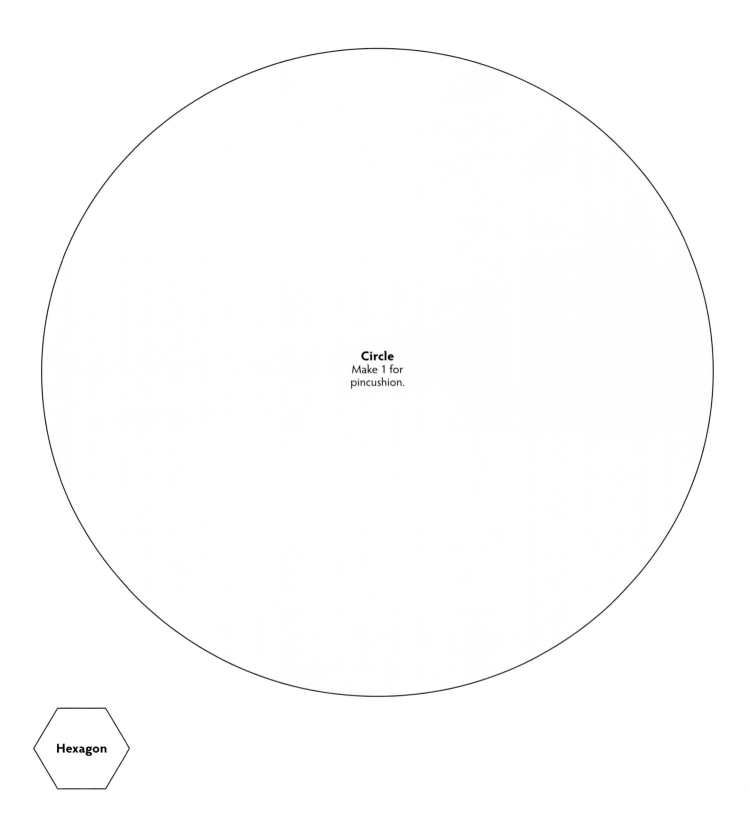

Circle
Make 1 for
pincushion.

Hexagon

Banner Day Garland

Decorate for the holidays or other special occasions such as baby showers, housewarmings, or graduations with a garland that can be personalized to suit any event.

Finished size: 7½" × 81" (excluding tassels)

- ❋ Permanent-ink stamp pad in gray
- ❋ 5 eyelets in assorted colors
- ❋ Eyelet setting tool

Cutting

All measurements include ¼" seam allowances. Trace the garland and rosette patterns on page 41 onto cardstock or template plastic and cut them out. Use the templates to cut the garland and rosette pieces from the fabrics indicated below.

From *each* of the 5 fat eighths, cut:

2 garland pieces (10 total)

From the muslin, using pinking shears or a pinking blade, cut:

5 strips, 1½" × 4"

From the scraps of assorted prints, cut a total of:

5 rosette pieces, cutting the curved edge with pinking shears*

From the ball trim, cut:

5 pieces, 7" long

*Instead of the scalloped rosettes, the featured project has three rosettes made with 1½" × 7" strips, one of whose long edges is cut with pinking shears or a pinking blade.

Assembling the Garland

Use a ¼" seam allowance and sew right sides together.

1. Sew two matching garland pieces together, leaving the top (straight) edge open. Clip into each inner point and notch the outer curves. Trim across the bottom point to reduce bulk. Turn right side out and press flat. Make five garland shapes.

Materials

Fat eighths measure 9" × 22".

- ❋ 5 assorted fat eighths in pink, blue, and white for garland
- ❋ 10" × 10" square of muslin for word embellishments
- ❋ 2 strips, 2½" × 42", of red check for garland tie
- ❋ 5 scraps, 2" × 8" or larger, of assorted coordinating prints for rosettes
- ❋ 1 yard of ball trim, ½" wide
- ❋ 5 buttons, ¾" diameter or smaller, for embellishment
- ❋ 5 skeins of embroidery floss in coordinating colors for tassels
- ❋ Cardstock OR template plastic
- ❋ Pinking shears OR rotary cutter with pinking blade
- ❋ Alphabet OR word rubber stamps, about ¼" tall

Make 5 garland shapes.

2 Use rubber stamps to stamp the desired word or phrase on each muslin 1½" × 4" pinked strip. Position each muslin strip on a garland shape and topstitch the short ends in place.

Sew stamped muslin strips to garland shapes.

3 Sew the red check 2½" × 42" strips together to make one long strip. Press the seam allowances open. Fold the strip in half lengthwise and press; unfold. Fold each raw edge inward to meet at the pressed centerline, then fold in half on the centerline to prepare the garland tie. Press.

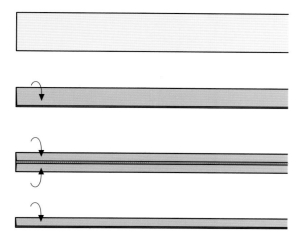

4 Referring to the diagram and evenly spacing the garland shapes, enclose the raw edges of the garland shapes within the folds of the garland tie. Pin in place. Insert the base of a 7" length of ball trim into the tie folds over the top of each garland shape. Topstitch close to the folded edges of the red check strip to secure the tie to the garland shapes and ball trim.

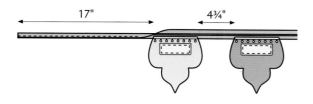

17"   4¾"

Embellish Until Your Heart's Content

More is always better when it comes to embellishing a project. Use pom-poms, rickrack, or ribbon to add detail to your garland. Instead of making the rosette, you can buy flowers from a craft store and glue in place.

Making and Adding the Embellishments

1 Use strong (or doubled) thread to sew a running stitch a scant ¼" from the straight edge of a rosette piece (or the nonpinked long edge of a 1½" × 7" strip). Pull up the thread ends to gather the piece into a rosette. Tie the thread ends tight and adjust the gathers as desired. Hand sew a button to the center of the rosette. Make five.

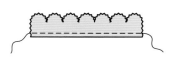

Make 5.

2 Hand sew each rosette onto a garland shape as indicated by the X on the pattern.

3 To make a tassel, remove the papers from one skein of floss. Cut two 10" pieces for the tie and loop. Lay the remainder of the skein on your work surface and place one of the 10" floss pieces across the center. Fold the remainder of the skein in half over the 10" floss piece. Tie the 10" piece tightly in a knot over the skein. Tie the ends in a knot to make

a hanger. Wrap the remaining 10" floss piece around the folded skein about ½" from the top knot. Tie in a knot. Trim the loops at the bottom to make a tassel. Trim it to the desired length. Make five tassels.

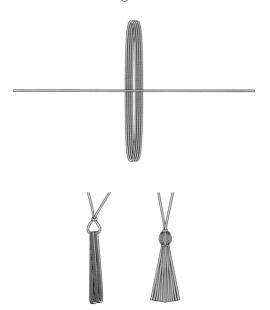

4 Poke a hole at the bottom of each garland piece as indicated by black dot on the pattern. Insert an eyelet from the front of the garland piece and use an eyelet setter to set it. Push the loop of a tassel through each hole. Tie in a lark's head knot to secure.

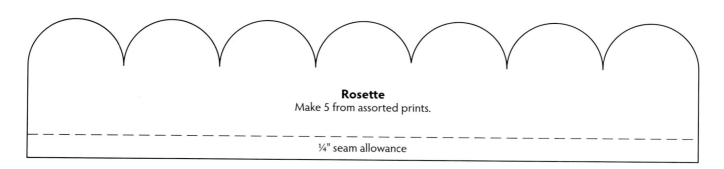

Rosette
Make 5 from assorted prints.

¼" seam allowance

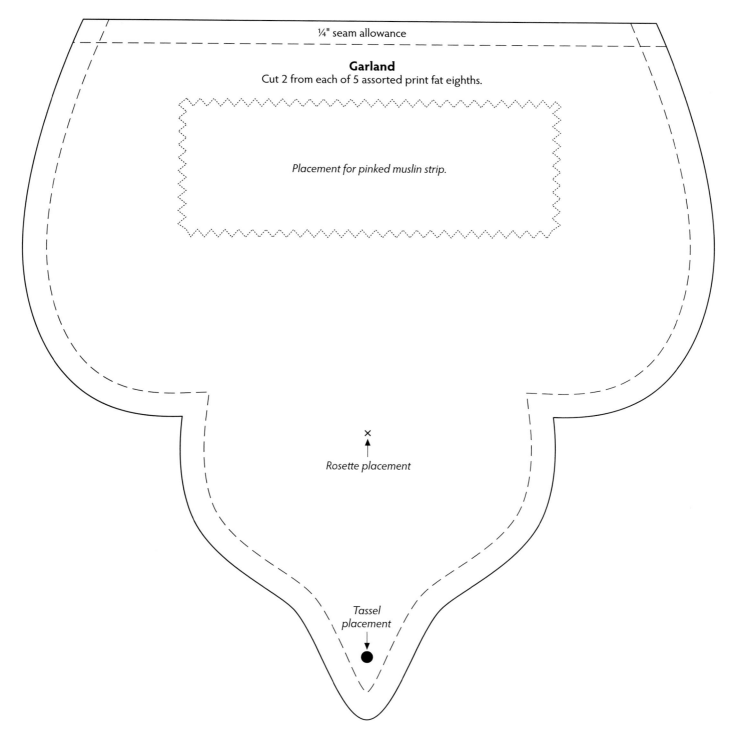

¼" seam allowance

Garland
Cut 2 from each of 5 assorted print fat eighths.

Placement for pinked muslin strip.

×

Rosette placement

Tassel placement

Large Gift Tags

Make personalized tags to accompany gifts or add a decorative touch on holidays or other special occasions. Let your fabric scraps shine, and let the merriment begin!

Finished Size: 2⅛" × 4¼" (excluding tie)

Materials

Yields 1 tag.

❊ Scrap of cotton fabric, at least 3" × 4", for pocket

❊ Scrap of selvage with word printed on it

❊ Scrap of fusible web as big as the selvage scrap

❊ Purchased manila shipping tag #4 (2⅛" × 4¼")
   OR heavyweight manila cardstock

❊ 1½" × 3" rectangle of light brown cardstock

❊ ¼ yard of string for tie

❊ Pinking shears OR rotary cutter with pinking blade

❊ Alphabet OR word rubber stamps, about ¼" tall

❊ Permanent-ink stamp pad in sepia

❊ Copy paper

Cutting

Trace the pocket pattern at right onto copy paper and cut it out. Use the template to cut the pocket from the fabric indicated below. If you're making your own tag, trace the tag pattern onto copy paper, cut it out, and use the template to cut a tag from heavyweight manila cardstock.

From the scrap of cotton fabric, cut:

1 pocket

Making the Tag

1 Fold the pocket on the fold line and press. Align the pocket, wrong side down, with the bottom three edges of the tag and machine sew in place ¼" from the bottom three edges.

2 Fuse the scrap of fusible web onto the back of the selvage piece. Use pinking shears or a pinking blade to cut around the desired word. Refer to the photo on page 42 to fuse the word to the bottom of the pocket.

3 Stamp the desired word on the brown 1½" × 3" cardstock rectangle. Tuck this rectangle into the pocket.

4 Thread both ends of the string into the hole at the top of the tag. Bring the thread ends through the loop and tighten to make a lark's head knot.

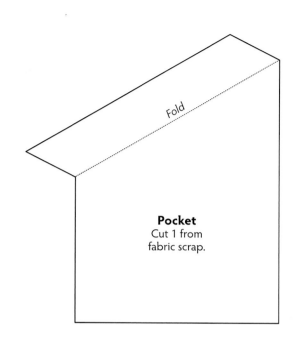

Pocket
Cut 1 from fabric scrap.

Fold

Tag
Cut 1 from heavyweight cardstock.

Project Pouch

Store your project pieces in a zippered hexie pouch that's ideal for keeping small items secure. Hint: make a few extra pouches because your friends are sure to want one too!

Finished Size: Approximately 7" × 8¼"

Materials

Yardage is based on 42"-wide fabric. Yields 1 pouch.

❋ ⅓ yard of coral print for pouch outside and lining

❋ Scrap of coordinating print for tab

❋ 10" × 25" piece of thin batting

❋ Zipper, 10" long

❋ ¼ yard of leather cord, ⅛" diameter

❋ 2 wooden beads, ¾" diameter and ½" diameter

❋ Cardstock *OR* template plastic

❋ Scrap of fabric selvage with word printed on it (optional)

❋ Decorative charm (optional)*

*The project shown features Zipper Pull Charms available from Poppie Cotton. See "Resources," page 80.

Cutting

All measurements include ¼" seam allowances. Trace the whole hexagon and half hexagon patterns on page 48 onto cardstock or template plastic and cut them out. Use the templates to cut the shapes from the fabric indicated below.

From the coral print, cut:

2 hexagons

4 half hexagons

From the scrap of coordinating print, cut:

1 piece, 2½" × 3"

From the batting, cut:

1 hexagon

2 half hexagons

From the leather cord, cut:

1 piece, 7" long"

Assembling the Pouch Top

Use a ¼" seam allowance and sew right sides together unless otherwise specified.

1 Place one coral half hexagon on your surface right side up as shown. Align the zipper, right side up, with the long edge of the half hexagon. Then place the batting and a second coral half hexagon right side down on top of the first two pieces. Sew together through all layers on the left side.

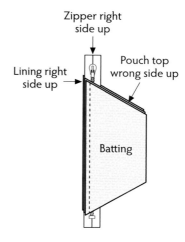

2 Fold the fabric and batting pieces over the seam allowance of the zipper and press. Topstitch in place.

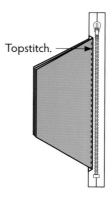

3 Repeat steps 1 and 2 to sew the remaining half hexagon pieces to the opposite side of the zipper to make the pouch top.

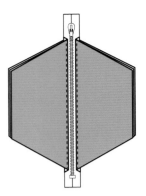

4 Unzip the zipper so the pull is below the edge of the hexagons. Stitch across each end of the zipper tape several times to secure, then trim the zipper ends off.

5 Fold the print 2½" × 3" piece in half lengthwise and press; unfold. Fold each raw edge inward to meet at the pressed centerline, then fold in half on the centerline. Press. Topstitch close to the edge to complete the tab.

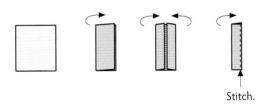

Stitch.

6 Fold the tab in half and position the raw edges of the tab in the center of one edge of the pouch top. Baste the tab raw ends to the pouch top within the seam allowance.

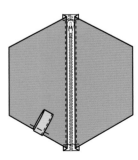

7 If desired, turn under the edges of the selvage scrap and position it on the pouch top, parallel to the zipper. Hand or machine sew in place.

8 Quilt the pouch top as desired. The featured project is machine quilted with parallel straight lines ½" apart.

Assembling the Pouch

1 Layer the coral whole hexagons right sides out with the batting in between. Quilt as desired to make the pouch bottom. The featured project is machine quilted with parallel straight lines ½" apart.

2 Unzip the zipper on the pouch top. With right sides together, layer the pouch top and bottom. Sew around all edges using a generous ¼" seam allowance. Trim across each corner to reduce bulk.

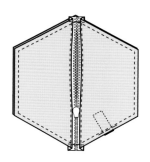

3 Turn the pouch right side out through the zipper opening and gently poke the corners out. Press flat. Topstitch ¼" from the edges.

4 Refer to the photo on page 44 to thread the leather cord through one of the zipper pull openings, then thread both ends through the wooden beads. Tie the ends in a knot. If desired, attach a decorative charm to the remaining opening of the zipper pull.

Make Your Own Key Charm Pull

Be creative when digging through your drawers to find beads to use as a key charm pull. They can be wood, porcelain, plastic, or resin. Thread the beads onto a ribbon or string and tie to your zipper. You could also make a tassel out of thin cuts of fabric, or even crochet yarn and tie it through the zipper.

Whole Hexagon (place on fold)
Cut 1 from batting.
Cut 2 from coral print.

Half Hexagon
Cut 2 from batting.
Cut 4 from coral print.

Patchwork Pin Minder

Mind your pins and needles with the prettiest pincushion ever! A touch of embroidery adds a special message to the sweet and simple patchwork design.

Finished Size: Approximately 7½" × 3½"

Materials

Yardage is based on 42"-wide fabric. Fat eighths measure 9" × 22".

* 1 fat eighth of light pink print for pincushion top and back

* Scraps of assorted prints for patchwork

* 9" × 15" piece of batting

* Embroidery floss in coral and light pink

* Embroidery needle

* Embroidery hoop

* Fine-point permanent pen *OR* Heartfelt Hexie Collection stamps and permanent-ink stamp pad*

* Polyester fiberfill and birdseed for stuffing

*The project shown features the Stamp & Stitch Heartfelt Hexie Collection stamps available from Poppie Cotton. See "Resources," page 80.

Cutting

All measurements include ¼" seam allowances.

From the light pink print, cut:
1 square, 8" × 8"
1 piece, 4½" × 8½"

From the scraps of assorted prints, cut:
12 squares, 1½" × 1½"

From the batting, cut:
1 square, 8" × 8"
1 piece, 5" × 9"

Embroidering the Pincushion Top

Use two strands of embroidery floss unless otherwise stated. Refer to "Embroidery Stitches" on page 79 and the pattern on page 51 as needed.

1 Use a light box or sunny window to trace the embroidery design with a permanent pen onto the pink 8" square, centering the design. Or, if you're using the Heartfelt Hexie Collection stamps, stamp the design instead.

2 Layer the traced square over the batting 8" square and hoop together. Embroider the design with coral embroidery floss, using lazy daisy stitches and French knots for the leaves and petals and using backstitches for the stems, blooms, and words. Chain stitch the outer hexagon and backstitch the inner hexagon.

3 Trim the embroidered square to 5½" wide and 4½" tall, including seam allowances. Carefully trim away the excess batting close to the outer hexagon.

Assembling the Pincushion

Use a ¼" seam allowance and sew right sides together. Press the seam allowances in the directions indicated by the arrows.

1 Lay out the assorted print 1½" squares in four rows as shown. Sew together the pieces in each row. Join the rows to make a 12-patch unit measuring 3½" × 4½", including seam allowances.

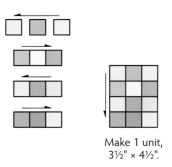

Make 1 unit,
3½" × 4½".

2 Join the embroidered 4½" × 5½" piece and the 12-patch unit to make the pincushion top.

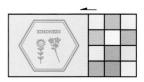

Make the pincushion top,
8½" × 4½".

3   Layer the pincushion top over the batting 5" × 9" piece. Use light pink floss to hand quilt as desired over the pincushion top. The featured project is stitched inside and outside the embroidered hexagons and with diagonal lines through the squares of the 12-patch unit. Trim the batting even with the pincushion top.

4   Sew the pincushion top and pink 4½" × 8½" piece together around all edges, leaving a 2" opening on one long edge.

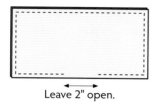

Leave 2" open.

5   Turn right side out and press flat. Stuff with birdseed and top off with polyester fiberfill. Slip stitch the opening closed.

Embroidery Key

- - - - - Backstitch

ᗡᗡᗡᗡ Chain stitch

● French knot

⌒ Lazy daisy

KINDNESS

Embroidery pattern

Scalloped-Edge Gift Box

What's in the box? Any small surprise is sure to be right at home in this charming container. Simple to construct, the fabric-covered boxes lend a cheery handmade touch.

Finished size: 3" wide × 3" deep × 3½" high

Materials

Yardage is based on 42"-wide fabric. Yields 1 box.

❋ 10" × 10" square of yellow, blue, or pink print for box

❋ 9" × 9" square of paper-backed fusible web

❋ 8½" × 11" sheet of heavy cardstock for box

❋ Hot-glue gun and glue sticks

❋ ⅓ yard of rickrack, ½" wide, *OR* ball trim, ½" wide (optional)

❋ Items for optional rosette embellishment:
  • Scrap of fabric, at least 2" × 8"
  • White button, ¾" diameter
  • Pinking shears *OR* rotary cutter with pinking blade

Assembling the Box

1 Following the manufacturer's instructions, center and fuse the fusible web 9" square to the wrong side of the print square. Remove the paper backing.

2 Use a pencil to trace the box pattern on page 54 onto copy paper and cut it out to make a template. Trace the template onto the heavy cardstock. Place the cardstock, traced side up, on the fusible side of the fabric square. Fuse in place, then let cool.

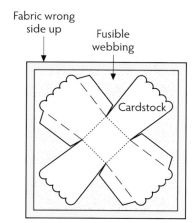

Fabric wrong side up   Fusible webbing   Cardstock

3 Cut through all layers on the outer solid lines. Fold on the dashed lines. Erase the pencil lines if desired. Fold into a box shape and hot glue the tabs in place to the back of the adjacent edges.

4 If desired, hot glue rickrack or ball trim to the outside of the box, folding under the outer raw edge. For the optional rosette, cut a 1½" × 7" strip, cutting one of the long edges with pinking shears or a pinking blade. Refer to Step 1 of "Making and Adding the Embellishments" in the Banner Day Garland instructions on page 40 to make the rosette and add the button.

Just the Beginning!

Rickrack, pom-poms, and rosettes are just a few of the ways you can decorate these gift boxes. Consider fusing a contrasting appliqué to one side (before assembling the box) or gluing fringe or ribbon around the top. Have fun making them unique!

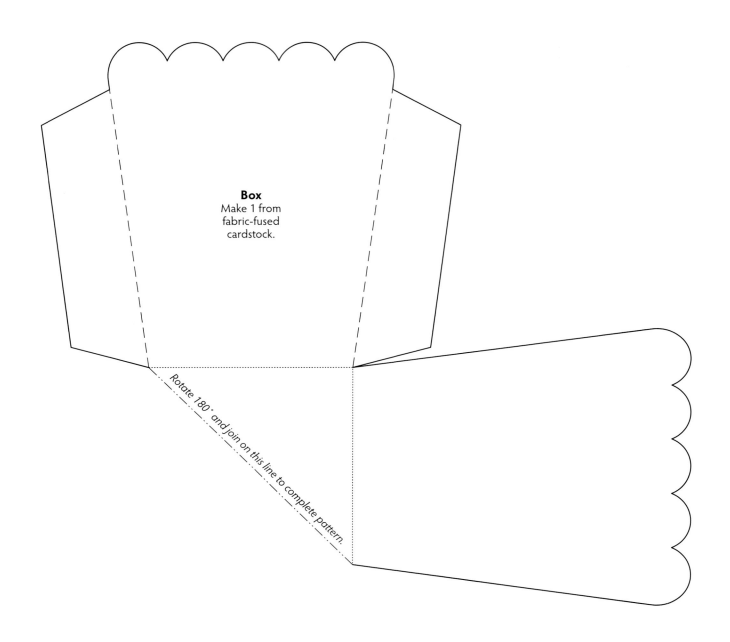

Box
Make 1 from
fabric-fused
cardstock.

Rotate 180° and join on this line to complete pattern.

Sweet Nothings Pouch

Transform bits of fabric into a handy pouch for small keepsakes. A few beads embellish the zipper pull, putting a fun finishing touch on your stylish little bag.

Finished size: 8" × 6"

Materials

Yardage is based on 42"-wide fabric. Yields 1 pouch.

❋ ⅓ yard of main print for pouch outside and lining

❋ Scrap of coordinating print, at least 3" × 10", for zipper ends and tab

❋ 8" × 19" piece of batting

❋ Zipper, 10" long

❋ ¼ yard of leather cord, ⅛" diameter

❋ 2 wooden beads, ½" diameter

❋ Scrap of fabric selvage with word printed on it (optional)

❋ Decorative charm (optional)*

The projects shown feature Zipper Pull Charms available from Poppie Cotton. See "Resources," page 80.

Cutting

All measurements include ¼" seam allowances.

From the main print, cut:
  4 pieces, 7" × 9"

From the coordinating print, cut:
  3 pieces, 2" × 3"

From the batting, cut:
  2 pieces, 7" × 9"

From the leather cord, cut:
  1 piece, 7" long"

Assembling the Pouch

Use a ¼" seam allowance and sew right sides together unless otherwise specified.

1 Fold each coordinating print 2" × 3" piece in half lengthwise and press; unfold. Fold the raw edges inward to meet at the pressed centerline, then fold in half on the centerline. Press. On one of the pieces,

topstitch close to the edge to make a tab. Do not sew the other two pieces yet.

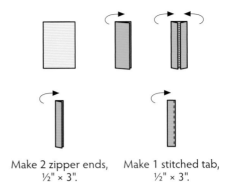

Make 2 zipper ends, ½" × 3".   Make 1 stitched tab, ½" × 3".

2 Cut the zipper to 8" long. Enclose the cut ends with the remaining prepared pieces from step 1 and topstitch in place to bind the zipper ends.

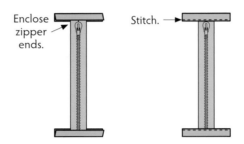

Enclose zipper ends.   Stitch.

3 Place one main print 7" × 9" piece on your work surface right side up. Align the zipper, right side up, with the left edge of the piece. Then place a second main print 7" × 9" piece and a batting 7" × 9" piece right side down on top of the first two pieces. Sew together through all layers on the left side.

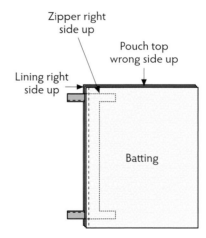

Zipper right side up
Pouch top wrong side up
Lining right side up
Batting

4 Fold the fabric and batting pieces over the seam allowance of the zipper and press. Topstitch in place.

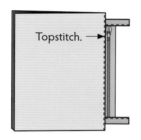

Topstitch. →

5 Repeat steps 3 and 4 to sew the remaining fabric and batting 7" × 9" pieces to the opposite side of the zipper.

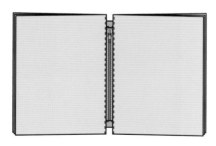

6 Unzip the zipper halfway. Fold the tab from step 1 in half and position it on the outside of the pouch, 1½" from the zipper. Baste in place to the outside fabric and batting only.

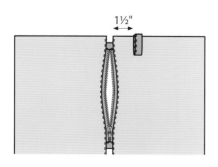

1½"

7 If desired, turn under the edges of the selvage scrap and position on the pouch top below the tab. Hand or machine sew in place to the outside fabric and batting only.

8 Fold the pouch so the outside fabrics are right sides together and the lining sides are right sides together. Use clips to secure the seams to line up. Note: When matching seams, make sure the zipper teeth go toward the lining. Stitch around the outside edges with a ½" seam allowance, leaving a 2" opening in the bottom of the lining. Be careful when going across the zipper. Sew up close to the zipper tabs but do not sew over them.

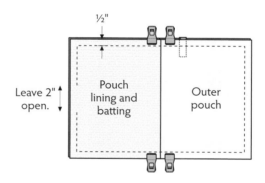

½"

Leave 2" open.

Pouch lining and batting

Outer pouch

9 Trim across the bottom corners to reduce bulk. Turn the pouch right side out through the opening in the lining. Fold in the edges of the lining opening and topstitch the opening closed. Push the lining inside of the pouch and press flat.

10 Referring to the photo on page 55, thread the leather cord through one opening, then thread both ends through the wooden beads. Tie the ends in a knot. If desired, attach a decorative charm to the remaining opening of the zipper pull.

Sweet Little Sentiments

Create a parcel that's sure to please, and stitch a special message on a wee woolen note card to tuck inside. It's the perfect design for Valentine's Day—or any day!

Finished size: Envelope, 4¼" × 5"
Finished Size: Heart, 3⅛" × 4½"

Materials

Yields 1 heart and envelope.

* 7" × 7" square of pink *OR* red felted wool for envelope outside
* 5" × 6" piece of white *OR* pink print for envelope lining
* 5" × 8" piece of pink, red, *OR* ivory felted wool for hearts
* Scraps of pink, red, and green felted wool for leaf and circle appliqués
* 1 red *OR* pink button, ½" diameter, for embellishment
* 1 red *OR* pink button, ⅜" diameter, for embellishment
* Embroidery floss in pink and red
* Chenille needle, size #20 or #22
* Chalk marker
* 3½" × 4½" piece of heavyweight cardstock for stabilizer
* Cardstock *OR* template plastic
* Freezer paper

Cutting

Trace the envelope lining pattern and cardboard insert pattern on page 62 onto cardstock or template plastic and cut them out. Use the template to cut the pieces from the materials indicated below.

From the white or pink print, cut:

1 envelope lining

From the heavyweight cardstock, cut:

1 cardboard insert

Making the Envelope and Heart

Use two strands of embroidery floss unless otherwise stated. Refer to "Embroidery Stitches" on page 79 and the pattern as needed.

1 Referring to "Wool Appliqué" on page 78, trace the patterns for the envelope, hearts, and appliqués on pages 61 and 62 onto the freezer paper and prepare the wool shapes.

2 Turn under ¼" on the side and top edges of the white or pink envelope lining; press. Position the envelope lining on the wool envelope, about ¼" from the top point. Hand sew the side and top edges in place.

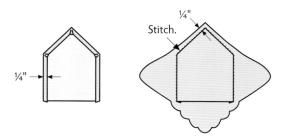

3 Insert the cardboard in the bottom edge of the envelope lining.

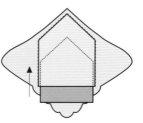

Insert cardboard.

4 Fold the side and bottom points of the envelope on the fold lines. Hand stitch in place where they overlap (sewing through the top three layers of wool only).

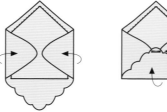

Secure with hand stitches.

5 Stack the ½" and ⅜" buttons and hand sew to the overlap where you already stitched. Sew a running stitch on the upper edges of the envelope. Blanket stitch the curved bottom flap to the wool below.

6 Use a chalk marker to trace the desired word embroidery pattern on page 61 onto one heart. Pin the two hearts together and then sew a running stitch around the outside of the hearts to secure. Backstitch the words. Use a French knot to dot the *i* in *Be Mine*.

7 Position the desired leaves and circles on the heart. Whipstitch just the inner point of each leaf in place, then make a cross-stitch in the center of the circles to secure.

Be Mine   XOXO

Love

Embroidery Key

----- Backstitch

● French knot

Embroidery patterns

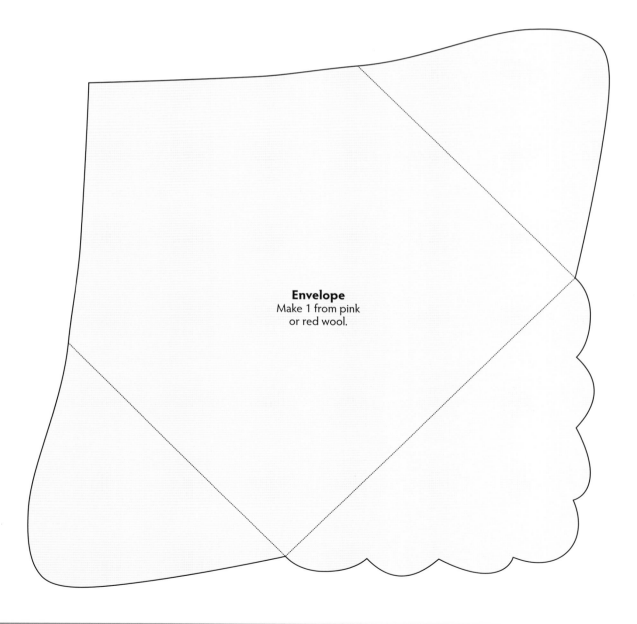

Envelope
Make 1 from pink
or red wool.

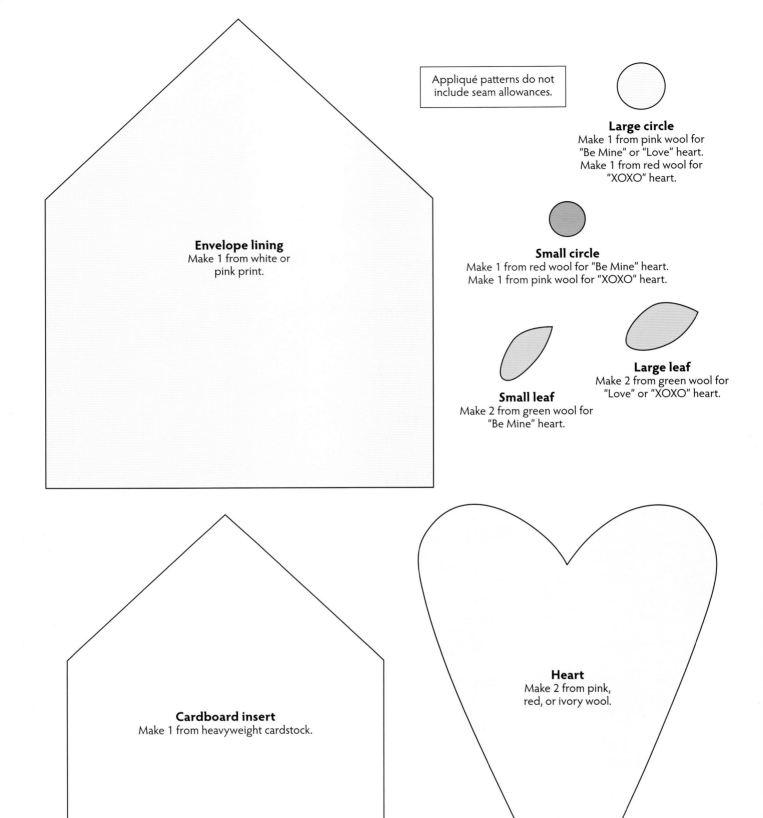

Appliqué patterns do not include seam allowances.

Envelope lining
Make 1 from white or pink print.

Large circle
Make 1 from pink wool for "Be Mine" or "Love" heart.
Make 1 from red wool for "XOXO" heart.

Small circle
Make 1 from red wool for "Be Mine" heart.
Make 1 from pink wool for "XOXO" heart.

Large leaf
Make 2 from green wool for "Love" or "XOXO" heart.

Small leaf
Make 2 from green wool for "Be Mine" heart.

Cardboard insert
Make 1 from heavyweight cardstock.

Heart
Make 2 from pink, red, or ivory wool.

Wraparound Sewing Caddy

Gather up your little sewing notions and give them a happy home. So pretty and practical, the caddy keeps things tidy and makes your sewing time all the more fun!

Finished size: Approximately 2½" diameter × 7½" wide (closed)

Materials

Yardage is based on 42"-wide fabric. Fat eighths measure 9" × 22".

* ¼ yard *total* of assorted prints in blue, pink, coral, and white for sewing caddy outside

* 3" × 11" piece of coral print for borders on sewing caddy outside

* 1 fat eighth of white floral for sewing caddy inside

* 1 fat eighth of aqua print for sewing caddy ends

* 8" × 11" piece of batting

* ⅞ yard of ribbon, ⅝" wide, for ties

* 1 pink button, ½" diameter, for embellishment

* 1 blue button, ⅜" diameter, for embellishment

* 3" × 5" piece of heavyweight cardstock for sewing caddy ends

* Cardstock *OR* template plastic

Cutting

All measurements include ¼" seam allowances.
Trace the circle patterns on page 67 onto cardstock or template plastic and cut them out. Use the templates to cut the circles from the materials indicated below.

From the assorted prints, cut:
  15 squares, 2½" × 2½"

From the coral print, cut:
  2 strips, 1¼" × 10½"

From the white floral, cut:
  1 piece, 8" × 11"

From the aqua print, cut:
  2 large circles

From the ribbon, cut:
  1 piece, 30" long

From the heavyweight cardstock, cut:
  2 small circles

Assembling the Sewing Caddy

Use a ¼" seam allowance and sew right sides together unless otherwise specified. Press the seam allowances in the directions indicated by the arrows.

1 Arrange the 15 assorted print 2½" squares in five rows. Sew together the pieces in each row. Join the rows to make a 15-patch unit.

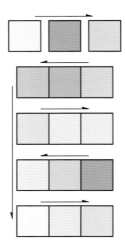

2 Sew the coral 1¼" pieces to the sides of the 15-patch unit to make the sewing caddy outside, which should measure 8" × 10½", including seam allowances.

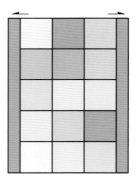

Make 1 sewing caddy outside,
8" × 10½".

3 Fold the ribbon 30" length in half and baste to the center of one short edge of the sewing caddy outside.

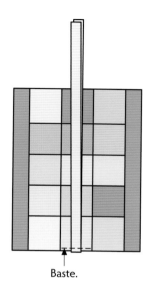

Baste.

4 Roll up and pin the ribbon to the center of the sewing caddy outside. On your work surface, place the batting 8" × 11" piece, white floral 8" × 11" backing piece (right side up), and sewing caddy outside (right side down). Sew together with a ¼" seam, leaving a 2" opening on one short end.

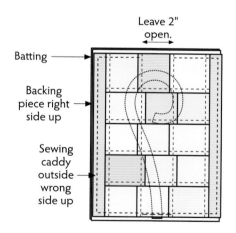

Leave 2"
open.

Batting

Backing
piece right
side up

Sewing
caddy
outside
wrong
side up

Creative Closures for Sewing Caddy

Instead of using ribbon to close your sewing caddy, use a small piece of elastic looped around a button. Put the elastic in place of the ribbon and move the buttons down lower so the elastic can loop around the buttons and stay taut when closed. You could also use a snap. Many colorful snaps are available at your favorite craft store.

6 Finger-press under a scant ¼" on one aqua print large circle. With a double-threaded needle, sew with a running stitch around the circle within the folded seam allowance. Place the cardboard small circle in the center and gently cinch up the stitches. Continue stitching to anchor the gathers and end the thread with a knot, making a yo-yo. Repeat with the remaining aqua print large circle and cardboard small circle.

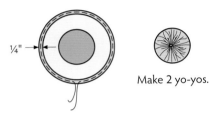

¼"

Make 2 yo-yos.

7 Align one edge of a yo-yo with the right side of the sewing caddy outside (on the opposite end from the ribbon tie). Start sewing with a blind stitch.

5 Clip across the corners to reduce bulk. Turn right side out and press flat. Hand stitch the opening closed. Topstitch the edge with the ribbons close to the edge. Stack the ½" and ⅜" buttons and hand sew on the center of the edge with the ribbon.

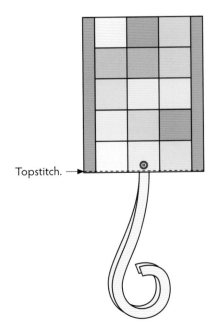

Topstitch. →

8 Continue sewing the sewing caddy outside to the yo-yo until you reach where you started sewing (the sewing caddy outside will extend beyond the yo-yo). Repeat to attach the remaining yo-yo to the opposite end of the sewing caddy outside.

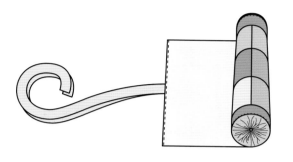

Small circle
Make 2 from heavyweight cardstock.

Large circle
Make 2 from aqua print.

Sweet Messages Bookmarks

A favorite book deserves a fabulous bookmark, don't you think? Create a lovely one for yourself or a friend with a patchwork design bearing its own simple message.

Finished Size: 2½" × 7½" (excluding loop)

Materials

Yardage is based on 42"-wide fabric. Fat eighths measure 9" × 22". Yields 1 bookmark.

* 1 fat eighth of white print for bookmark front and back

* Scraps, at least 1" × 3", of 5 assorted coordinating prints for bottom of bookmark

* Scrap of selvage with word printed on it

* 3" × 8" piece of thin cotton batting

* 5" × 5" square of coral felted wool for strawberry loop (optional)

* 5" × 5" square of green felted wool for stem on strawberry loop (optional)

* Embroidery floss in green and pink plus desired colors for bookmark embroidery

* ¼ yard of leather cord, ⅛" wide

* ⅛ yard of pink ribbon, ⅛" wide, for strawberry loop (optional)

* Fine-point permanent pen *OR* Farmhouse Monogram Collection stamps and permanent-ink stamp pad*

* Chenille needle, size #20 or #22

* Embroidery needle

* Freezer paper (optional)

*The project shown features the Stamp & Stitch Farmhouse Monogram Collection stamps available from Poppie Cotton. See "Resources," page 80.

Cutting

All measurements include ¼" seam allowances.

From the white print, cut:
1 piece, 3" × 8"
1 piece, 3" × 5"

From the assorted print scraps, cut:
5 pieces, 1" × 3"

From the selvage scrap, cut:
1 piece, 1" × 3"

From the leather cord, cut:
1 piece, 5" long

Assembling the Bookmark

Use a ¼" seam allowance and sew right sides together unless otherwise specified. Press the seam allowances in the directions indicated by the arrows.

1   Using a light box or sunny window, trace the desired letters on page 71 and then trace one or more of the embroidery designs on page 71 with a permanent pen onto the white print 3" × 5" piece, centering the design. Or if you're using the Farmhouse Monogram Collection stamps, stamp the letters and embroidery design instead.

2   Referring to the photo on page 68, embroider the design using the desired floss colors.

3   With the fabric right side up, align the top three edges of the stamped piece with the batting 3" × 8" piece. Position a print 1" × 3" piece right side down on the white print piece with the bottom edges aligned. Sew together through all layers, then press the print piece open. This process is called quilt-as-you-go.

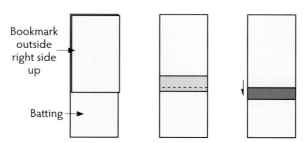

4   Using the selvage 1" × 3" piece and remaining print 1" × 3" pieces, continue adding pieces in the quilt-as-you-go manner until the batting piece is covered. Press well.

Make 1 unit,
3" × 8".

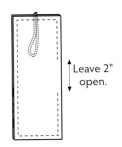

6 Layer the white print 3" × 8" piece with the bookmark top (right sides together) and sew around all edges, leaving a 2" opening.

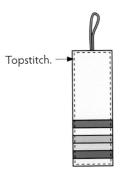

Leave 2" open.

7 Trim across the corners to reduce bulk, then turn right side out. Press. Topstitch around the outside edges to complete the bookmark.

Topstitch. →

Making the Strawberry Loop

Use two strands of embroidery floss unless otherwise stated. Refer to "Embroidery Stitches" on page 79 and the pattern as needed.

1 Referring to "Wool Appliqué" on page 78, trace the strawberry and stem patterns at right onto the freezer paper and prepare the wool shapes.

2 Place the green wool stem on the top of the coral wool strawberry and the green wool reversed stem on top of the coral wool reversed strawberry. Whipstitch the stem to each strawberry. Place the stem/strawberry units wrong sides together. Fold the 4½"-long pink ribbon in half. Sandwich the raw ends of the ribbon between the stem portions.

5 Fold the leather 5" cord in half and place the raw ends in the center of the top of the bookmark. Baste in place.

Baste.

3 Machine stitch across the top of the stems to secure the ribbon. Use pink floss to blanket stitch around the edges of the strawberry units and cross-stitch Xs on each strawberry for seeds. Tie the loop to the leather cord of the bookmark with a lark's head knot.

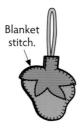

Blanket stitch.

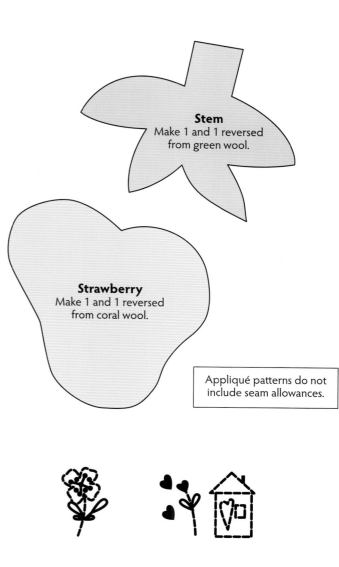

Stem
Make 1 and 1 reversed from green wool.

Strawberry
Make 1 and 1 reversed from coral wool.

Appliqué patterns do not include seam allowances.

Embroidery patterns

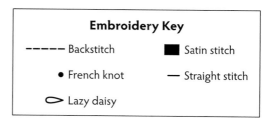

Embroidery Key

- - - - - Backstitch	▪ Satin stitch
● French knot	— Straight stitch
⌒ Lazy daisy	

Mushroom Pincushion

Stitch a whimsical pattern that'll make you smile! The design is so enchanting, your pins will sparkle atop the pincushion like dewdrops in a fairyland forest.

Finished size: Approximately 3½" diameter

Materials

* 10" × 10" square of pink print for large mushroom cap

* 7" × 9" piece of green felted wool for pincushion top and grass around mushrooms

* 6" × 10" piece of aqua print for mushroom stems

* 6" × 10" piece of coral print for small mushroom cap

* Scraps of red and coral felted wool for strawberries

* ⅓ yard of green ball trim, ½" wide

* ⅝ yard of light pink ball trim, ¼" wide

* ¼ yard of ivory crocheted lace trim, ¼" wide

* Embroidery floss in coral, fuchsia, green, pink, and red

* Cardstock OR template plastic

* Heavyweight cardstock

* Freezer paper

* Polyester fiberfill OR other pincushion stuffing

* Silicone cupcake mold with base approximately 3" diameter

* Hot-glue gun and glue sticks

Cutting

Trace the mushroom and small circle patterns on pages 76 and 77 onto cardstock or template plastic and cut them out. Use the template to cut the pieces from the materials indicated below.

From the green wool, cut:
2 strips, ¾" × 4"

1 large circle

From the pink print, cut:
4 large mushroom caps

1 large mushroom center

From the aqua print, cut:
2 large mushroom stems

2 small mushroom stems

From the coral print, cut:
4 small mushroom caps

1 small mushroom center

From the heavyweight cardstock, cut:
1 small circle

From the ¼"-wide ball trim, cut:
1 piece, 10½" long

1 piece, 8" long

From the crocheted lace trim, cut:
1 piece, 4" long

1 piece, 3" long

Assembling the Pincushion

Use two strands of embroidery floss unless otherwise stated. Refer to "Embroidery Stitches" on page 79 and the pattern as needed.

1 Referring to "Wool Appliqué" on page 78, trace the patterns for the strawberry appliqués and large circle on page 77 onto the freezer paper and prepare the wool shapes.

2 Referring to the diagram for placement, position the red and coral wool strawberries on the top of the green wool circle and pin in place. Use matching or contrasting floss to sew a running stitch around the edge of each strawberry to secure. Use matching or contrasting floss to sew several French knots for seeds on each strawberry. Use green floss to sew lazy daisy stitches at the top of each strawberry for stems. Sew featherstitch lines radiating out from the center. At the tip of each featherstitch, sew a French knot in coral, pink, or red.

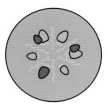

Appliqué and embroidery placement

4 Gather the threads and stuff the center of the circle with stuffing. Continue to stuff firmly and insert the small heavyweight cardboard circle. Tighten the stitches, and then secure with a knot.

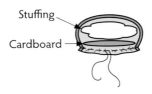

Stuffing

Cardboard

5 Hot glue the bottom of the pincushion into the silicone cupcake mold.

Assembling the Mushrooms

Use an ⅛" seam allowance and sew right sides together unless otherwise specified. Use a very short stitch length because you're using such a narrow seam allowance.

1 Sew together two large mushroom cap pieces along one side edge. Press the seam allowances in one direction. Make two pairs, pressing seam allowances in the same direction on each so they will abut when the pairs are joined.

Make 2 mushroom cap pairs.

2 Join the pairs of large mushroom cap pieces along the top curved edges to make the mushroom cap.

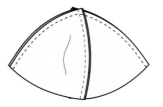

Make 1 mushroom cap.

Pretty, Pretty Pins

We make custom pins for our pincushions by using E6000 to glue charms to the tops of pins. You can find some of the cutest little charms on Etsy.

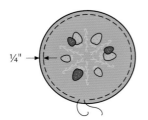

3 Use a doubled thread and ¼"-long stitching to sew a running stitch ¼" from the outside edge of the circle.

¼"

3 Sew the mushroom cap to the large mushroom center, leaving a 1" opening for turning.

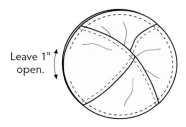

Leave 1" open.

4 Turn the mushroom cap right side out and stuff firmly. Hand stitch the opening closed. Hand stitch the 10½" length of ball trim around the mushroom cap.

5 Sew together the two large mushroom stem pieces along the sides and bottom.

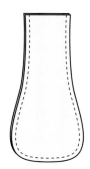

Make 1 mushroom stem.

6 Turn the mushroom stem right side out and stuff firmly. Hand stitch the top of the stem to the bottom of the large mushroom cap. To disguise any stitching or stuffing that's poking out, gather and sew or hot glue the 4" length of the crocheted lace trim around the top of the stem.

7 Using small mushroom pieces, an 8" piece of ball trim, and a 3" piece of crocheted lace trim, repeat steps 1–6 to make the small mushroom. If desired, stitch a flower with lazy daisies and a French knot in each quadrant of the pincushion top, referring to the photo above as needed.

8 Make ⅝"-long clips into each green wool ¾" × 4" piece, snipping them about ¼" apart.

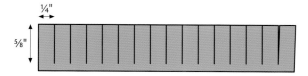

¼"

⅝"

Make 1 grass section.

9 Hand sew the large and small mushrooms to the top of the pincushion. Wrap the clipped green grass pieces from step 8 around the base of each mushroom and sew or hot glue in place. Wrap the ½" green ball trim around the top edge of the silicone cupcake mold and hot glue in place.

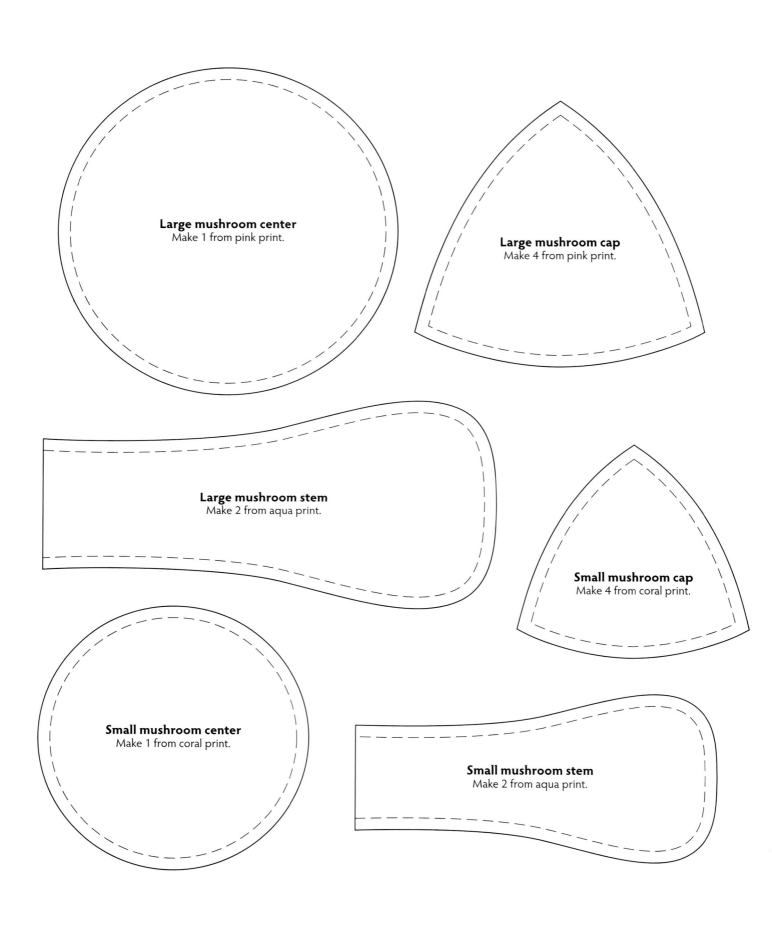

Large mushroom center
Make 1 from pink print.

Large mushroom cap
Make 4 from pink print.

Large mushroom stem
Make 2 from aqua print.

Small mushroom cap
Make 4 from coral print.

Small mushroom center
Make 1 from coral print.

Small mushroom stem
Make 2 from aqua print.

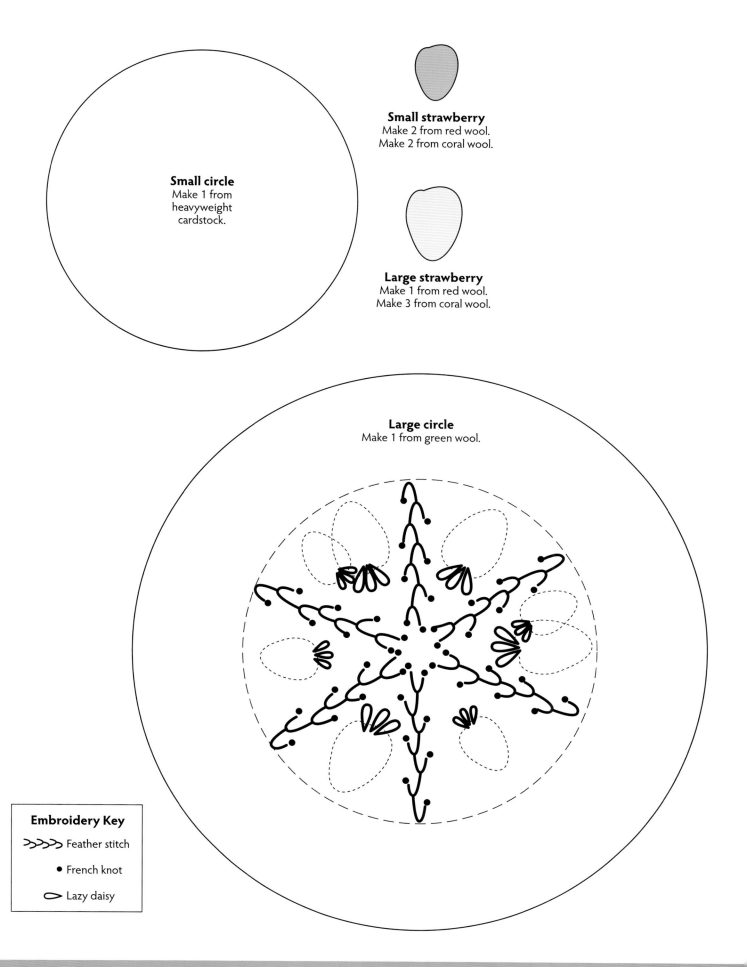

Small circle
Make 1 from
heavyweight
cardstock.

Small strawberry
Make 2 from red wool.
Make 2 from coral wool.

Large strawberry
Make 1 from red wool.
Make 3 from coral wool.

Large circle
Make 1 from green wool.

Embroidery Key

>>>>> Feather stitch

• French knot

◠ Lazy daisy

Special Techniques

In this section you'll find information on wool appliqué, embroidery stitches, and English paper piecing to guide you as you create the projects in this book.

Wool Appliqué

Felted wool doesn't fray. For that reason, it's a time-saving, raw-edge alternative to appliquéing with cotton fabrics. First, trace each shape onto the dull side of freezer paper, leaving at least ½" between shapes. Cut out each shape roughly ¼" around the drawn lines. Then use a warm dry iron to press the freezer-paper shapes, shiny side down, onto the wool. Cut through the fabric and freezer paper on the drawn lines. Each freezer-paper shape can be reused several times.

Referring to the photo and pattern for your project, position the appliqués on the background piece and baste or pin in place. Stitch the pieces in place with a whipstitch or blanket stitch, then add embroidered details as desired. Embroidery illustrations are shown on page 79.

English Paper Piecing

English paper piecing (or EPP) is all about wrapping fabric around a paper shape before sewing the pieces together to create complicated designs, such as hexagon shapes. The piecing is done by hand, so it's the perfect project to take along while traveling.

1 Precut papers are available in many shapes and sizes at your local quilt shop or from Paper Pieces (PaperPieces.com). To make your own paper pieces, trace the finished size of the pattern onto sturdy paper and cut out carefully on the drawn lines.

2 To prepare shapes, position a paper piece on the wrong side of a fabric piece. Trim the fabric, leaving ¼" around the paper piece. Wrap the seam allowances to the back of the paper and secure with water-soluble fabric glue.

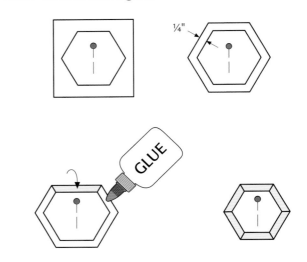

3 To join shapes, place two prepared shapes right sides together. Wonder Clips from Clover are great for holding the shapes together without pinning. Whipstitch a pair of edges together with tiny stitches, making a knot at each corner. Finger-press the pieces open and add the remaining shapes in the same manner. Press with a dry iron before removing the papers.

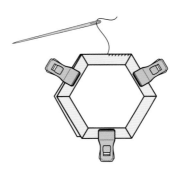

Embroidery Stitches

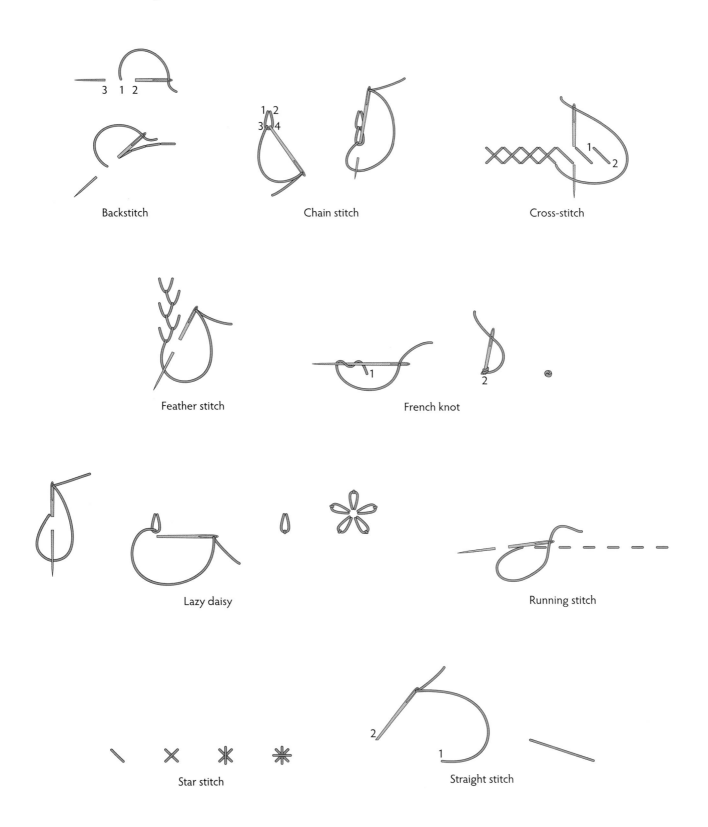

Backstitch

Chain stitch

Cross-stitch

Feather stitch

French knot

Lazy daisy

Running stitch

Star stitch

Straight stitch

Resources

Look for cotton and wool fabrics, Zipper Pull Charms, and Stamp & Stitch collections by Poppie Cotton at your local quilt shop. Visit PoppieCotton.com and click on "Where to Buy" to find a list of retailers.

About the Authors

It began with the color pink, the love of flowers, and a passion for creating beautiful things. Designer Jina Barney and artist Lori Woods found their joy as they formed their company—Poppie Cotton. Together, they pour their hearts and souls into everything lovely and creative that makes up this new venture.

Lori began her illustrating journey at a young age, drawing and coloring paper dolls and selling them for 25 cents to fourth-grade friends. Through years of developing her skill and licensing her illustrations, she finally found her niche at Poppie Cotton. Lori loves putting in long hours and collaborating with her dear friend and business partner, Jina. Lori's husband, Patrick, is a major force in the business, and all three work tirelessly alongside one another.

Quilter, teacher, and clothing designer Jina carefully designs and beautifully details the quilts, small projects, and other works of art showcasing the sweet fabrics from Poppie Cotton. Each carefully crafted quilt or pattern that she creates for Poppie Cotton deserves a standing ovation. She has honed the creative skills that she learned during her childhood in Australia. Now, her polished and perfected style flourishes here in the United States.

The two artists work remotely (Lori from Washington, where the company is headquartered, and Jina from Utah). Visit PoppieCotton.com and follow them on social media.